W9-BVR-566

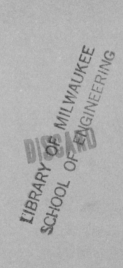

HIGH FLIERS

colorful kites from Japan

By Tadao Saito

JAPAN PUBLICATIONS, INC.

Published by
Japan Publications, Inc., Tokyo

Distributed by
Japan Publications Trading Company
1255 Howard St., San Francisco, Calif. 94103
175 Fifth Ave., New York, N.Y. 10010
P.O. Box 5030, Tokyo International, Tokyo, Japan

Library of Congress Catalog Card No. 74–75186
© 1969 by Japan Publications, Inc.
All rights reserved.

First printing: April 1969

Photographs by Ihei Misaki
Printed in Japan by Dai Nippon Printing Co., Ltd.

Contents

The author and his kite collection.

6

Preface

Countless kites of many shapes and colors sail against the leaden clouds. Already the day is darkening and the winter wind rattles the black boughs of the trees.

"Taro-chan, it's getting dark now. Come on home." The distant voice of a mother.

"I'm coming." The reluctant reply.

One kite glides down from the sky and travels homeward with a little boy.

"Hideo, supper."

"Yes m'am."

One more kite disappears.

"Well, Yukichi, how about walking home with your papa?"

"Okay."

And one by one the children, called home to the warmth of the family, haul their high-flying treasures from the darkening evening sky and leave.

Still one kite remains, even as the evening star begins to glimmer against the blue-black of night. When all his friends have gone home, only Chu-chan, the son of a nearby innkeeper, remains with his kite.

Evenings are the busiest hours for innkeepers, and no one from Chu-chan's family has the time to call him home for supper. Anyway, even if he returned, there would be no happy supper group waiting for him. Instead, he would only get in the way of all the bustling, busy people. That is why he remains alone in the dark playing with his friend, the kite.

"Hey, Chu-chan, cheer up; don't be sad. Let's have a good time together," the kite suddenly calls from its place in the sky.

"Okay, thanks."

"I know, Chu-chan. I'll show you a kite dance. Sing something to keep time."

"All right."

And as Chu-chan sings whatever children's song he knows, the kite dances a funny, jerky dance.

Shyosuke Yakko

"Hey, kite," says Chu-chan, "you're pretty good. That looks like fun."

"Well, not really. To tell the truth, the wind is cold up here; I'm actually only shivering."

The little boy and the kite continue playing till it is too dark for them to see each other.

*   *   *

Chu-chan, of course, grew up and today is busy with a regular job in the complicated world of adults, but he is also a collector and student of the Japanese kite, for which he maintains a deep affection. In his own words, "The common people created the kite, and although its colors and shapes may not be fine art, they represent the dreams of childhood and the homeland of the hearts of adults."

He also says that nostalgia is not his only reason for collecting kites: he feels a duty to save these lovely flying objects from becoming the victims of over-population and of too many automobiles, which, by making kite flying impossible, reduce the number of people producing kites.

He goes on to say, "A land rich with paper and bamboo, Japan, over many long ages, has developed many varieties of kites, some of which are the finest in the world. Because I would like to show children in other countries some of them, I have written this book."

By now, I suppose you have guessed that I am the Chu-chan of the little story.

Finally I should like to express many thanks to the following people for the advice and invaluable materials they lent me in the preparation of this book: Takizo Hayashi, Hikozo Ota, Ryosuke Saito, Shingo Modegi, Kazuya Sakamoto, Toshio Ishii, Jiro Sasaki. I am also grateful to Koji Okajima, The Nikkan Sports snapshot department, and the photography department of the Nihon Keizai Newspaper for providing photographic material.

TADAO SAITO

Flying seemingly into the sun. (*Photo by Koji Okajima*)

The Western and Japanese Attitudes to Kites

Always applying an intellectual, developmental, and categorizing intellect to things, Westerners are generally unable to enjoy kite flying for itself alone. As their children grow, they gradually want to produce kites that fly automatically without strings. From that stage they move to remote-control airplane models and later to the world of science fiction, flying saucers, and dreams of space ships crossing the vastness of the universe. Naturally the people of advanced nations, like the United States, consider simply

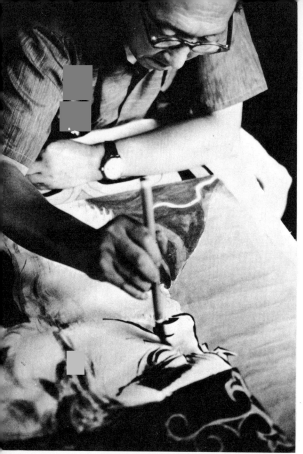

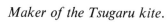

Maker of the Tsugaru kite.

Hikozo Ota painting his Ezo kite.

Other craftsmen decorating kite surfaces.

flying kites a child's pastime to be abandoned with the approach of manhood.

This being the case, the kites of the West are designed to fly well and nothing more. Lack of interest in the colors and shapes results from two facts: adults consider kites beneath their serious attention; most Western countries do not have large supplies of the resilient bamboo and tough, light Japanese paper that make possible creative variety in kite shapes and designs.

The Japanese, on the other hand, possessing these supplies in abundance, have created kite masterpieces, which on festival or congratulatory occasions, adults delight in showing off in contests of skill and displays of regional kite patterns and colors. Over the ages traditional fondness for this amusement has resulted in about 120–30 different kites that are not only beautiful but that also perform better than those built in any other country.

Because they appreciate and enjoy their kites as an end in themselves, the Japanese have never used them as a starting point from which to advance to science-fiction marvels. Perhaps this attitude can be attributed to the fate of a nation that, for the three hundred years of the Edo period, closed its doors to communications with other nations and lived entirely within the feudal structure of its own world. That is, perhaps the Japanese learned to enjoy fully what they had without dreaming of further development. Whether such an attitude is good or bad is beside the point, but it clearly explains why the Japanese love kites for their own beauty and pay little attention to functional advances. Perhaps the game room, where their pictures, colors, and forms can be displayed to best advantage, is as good a place for the Japanese kite as the open fields where they are sent aloft.

Kite History and Traditions

Although space forbids me to explain in detail the art of the woodblock-print makers of the eighteenth century, whose pictures greatly influenced the designs seen on kites even today, I should comment that many of the fine artists of Edo (Tokyo) of those days produced works which samurai and merchants alike bought and carried back as souvenirs to their native towns and villages, where the prints became models on which to develop kite designs of great local distinction. As the Edo-period government failed and Japan's isolation drew to a close, influences from many other lands—China, Southeast Asia, and India— began to work a great change in the nature of Japanese kites.

Foreign influence was particularly strong on the island of Kyushu, for many years Japan's leading window to the rest of the world.

Kites themselves are strongly linked with numerous year-round ceremonies and festivals and with religious methods of averting evil; their history is, consequently, an integral part of the life and knowledge of the Japanese people.

Eleventh-century records, using the same terms to describe banners and kites, clearly indicate that the kite was a military symbol. Furthermore, battle diaries of that and of later ages tell how military men employed kites to carry secret messages to allies, to carry food to troops besieged in castles, and to measure distances by the length of the kite string thereby gaining information enabling them to tunnel into enemy fortifications.

When the raging wars of the Middle Ages subsided and peace settled on the land, the people once again applied the kite to many aspects of daily life. For instance, in 1689, architect Kawamura Zuiken lifted workmen by kite to lay tiles on the great roof of the temple Zojo-ji. In contrast to such constructive applications of the kite, in 1712, arch thief Kakinoki Kinsuke tied himself to one, flew to the top roof of the dungeon of Nagoya Castle, and pilfered the pure gold scales from the dolphin ornaments on the ends of the ridge pole.

Records describe ancient New Year festivals in the Kanto District where shrines flew kites to the accompaniment of booming drums and pealing bells while seers interpreted the rising and inclining of the kite to foretell the harvests and fish catches of the year. A direct intuitive telepathic reaction on the part of the humans on the ground to movements of the upper air need not necessarily be branded as charlatanry. For instance, even today, fishermen in the Tohoku District fly kites to determine from the flow of the air and

Yuzawa

Iwai Ogi

Hirado Oniyocho

12

the currents the weather for the following day and, consequently, the danger or safety in putting out to sea. Learning from studying natural phenomena in this way helped Benjamin Franklin invent the lightning rod by flying a kite with a key tied to the string during a thunderstorm.

Another interesting kite story from the fishermen in the Tohoku District involves the string with which these men weave their own nets. For the sake of weight and compact shipping, the merchants usually sell string with a strong twist. The fishermen, too, have learned that buying less strongly twisted string than they need, giving it to the local children to use on kites, waiting till they have used it sufficiently to remove the twist, then taking it back for weaving gives them the correct length of soft untwisted string that will not break when caught on the corners of underwater rocks.

The fishermen of Chiba Prefecture, on the Pacific Coast, make a so-called sleeve kite in the shape of a jacket the men wear during the great fishing festivals. Each kite bears a family crest, and when the men put out to sea on long voyages they fly them. On returning they send the kites up again to signify to the families waiting on the shore that they have returned safe with a good catch. In contrast, families of fishermen living on the Japan Sea accompany their men to the shore and fly farewell kites that go with the ship as far as the string will stretch. When the men return, the families once again fly these kites in joyful welcome and thanks for a safely concluded trip. Interestingly enough, the flow of the southeast winds across the Japanese archipelago facilitates flying kites from ships on the Pacific side and from the land on the Japan Sea side.

As well as on the sea coasts of the country, kites are important parts of the agricultural life in inland Japan. Wherever one goes, each year farming villages hold summer and autumn festivals: at the former farmers fly kites with invocations for a good harvest

Tongari

Sode Jomon

Sanuki Daruma

13

painted on them and at the latter other kites with thanks for the good harvest past. Some of the autumn kites bear bunches of freshly cut grain tied to the tails both to show to the whole village the quality of the year's produce and to offer first fruits to the gods in heaven.

Another interesting rural custom takes place in the rice paddies after the harvest has been concluded. The young men of the village gather there to hold a contest of flying skill using kites with their own names painted in large letters on the fronts. The goal is to win the hand in marriage of the most beautiful daughter of the landowner. This young maiden, with her parents, must sit on grass mats spread in front of their gate and watch the proceedings.

Although ceremonies of this sort were common before World War II, now one must go deep into the mountains or to areas still unaffected by the wave of Western culture to find them.

On the twenty-first day following the birth of a child, Japanese parents must take him to the local shrine to give thanks and to pray for his growth and strength. In addition, two special holidays for children are held every year, one on March third and one on May fifth. The former, Girls' Day, is celebrated with a display of colorful dolls and with the drinking of sweetened sake and the eating of small diamond-shaped cakes, whereas a large carp streamer flying from a pole in the garden, a display of warrior dolls, and rice cakes wrapped in bamboo leaves are arranged to honor the latter, Boys' Day.

Naturally on these festival days, kites are often given as congratulatory articles to children: a shrine will present one to a child, or grandparents will give them to their grandchildren. One of the most popular of such kites is the one bearing the picture of Kintoki, a folk hero who, raised by bears in the moun-

Sagara Kintoki

Izumo Iwai

14

tains became the strongest man in Japan and later entered the service of the emperor. Other frequent gift kites include those decorated with the following designs: crane and tortoise (long life), carp (valiant fish that swims upstream in waterfalls), dragon (the symbol of prosperity because it can ascend to the heavens), Sugawara Michizane (a famous courtier who later came to represent the god of learning). Fukusuke or Daruma (the former a lucky dwarf, the latter the Japanese version of the Buddhist patriarch Bodhidharma, also supposed to bring luck).

Once long ago, in the town of Hachinohe in the Tohoku District of the main Japanese island, Honshu, lived a painter of votive pictures of the sort people offered to shrines in the hope of the fulfillment of a wish. For instance, a person with poor eyesight might donate a picture of eyes, one who wanted money would give a picture of an abacus, etc. On a certain day, the wife of a townsman came to the painter to request the following. "I want you to paint a picture of Kintoki so that my son will grow strong, but I want a kite, not an ordinary picture." The painter did as he was asked, and the wife took the kite to the shrine and flew it there. When asked the reason for her action, she replied. "Since the gods live in the heavens, I thought it would be a good idea to go directly to them instead of waiting for them to come to the shrine." After this story got around town, the painter was deluged with requests for kites. This is the origin of the famous Nambu kites, still produced in Hachinohe.

On the distant island Mishima in the Japan Sea, the people fly kites with pictures of ferocious demon faces well suited to their isolated home. Though they are called congratulatory kites, there is a strong element of the evil-averting talisman in them.

In houses where a son was born the previous year, the family and relatives gather while the grandfather paints a huge demon

Kyu Nambu

Sagara Ryu

Tenjin

15

kite —often the size of a moderate Japanese room. This they hang from the ceiling over the child, who can then see it everyday. The kite must be finished and up well before the New Year holiday. On the first of the year, the family once again meet, take down the great kite, and working all together, fly it in the cold, sea wind. Thus they cause all the danger of evil or disaster in the house to fly away into the sky and guarantee that the child will grow healthy and happy. This custom seems to persist in other parts of the nation where the old traditions are still honored. But hearing that a similar belief existed in Hagi, in West Japan, I traveled there to investigate. No one, however, could tell me anything about it. Even the priest in the local shrine said that evil-averting talismans were old fashioned and that today it would be wiser to devise ceremonies to avoid traffic accidents. Though many of the traditions connected with kites grew up in surroundings apparently inseparable from the daily lives of the people, today, Japan, as the leading Asian nation, is the scene of so much high-rise building and highway construction, the land of so many high-voltage towers and television and telephone cables, that kite-flying is all but impossible. Consequently, kite makers are vanishing.

Nevertheless, kites themselves, by some inexplicable miracle, continue to live. People who have fled the cities to reside in urban housing developments still buy and appreciate them. When these areas become overcrowded, kite sales fall, only to pick up again when a new, more distant settlement opens. According to department-store statistics, every five years kites sell well. I suspect that no amount of modernization can erase the fondness for the old things that the dogged, hang-on kite represents. As long as the Japanese are alive, somewhere someone will be flying them all through the year.

Magoji Semi

Oniyozu

Representative Kites

Fig. 1. *Edo Nishiki*

Fig. 3. *Tsugaru*

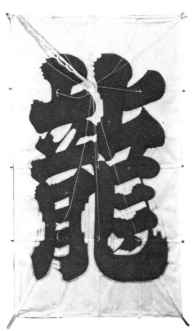

Fig. 2. *Edo Ryu*

Fig. 4. *Nambu*

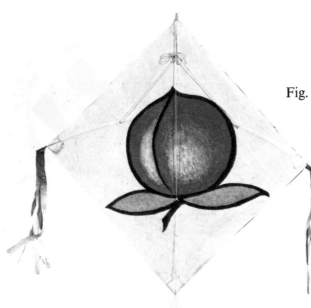

Fig. 5. *Ichimon Ten-hata*

Fig. 6. *Onna Berabo*

Fig. 7. *Aizu Dojin*

18

Fig. 8. *Oji Hibuse*

Fig. 9. *Sagami Abu*

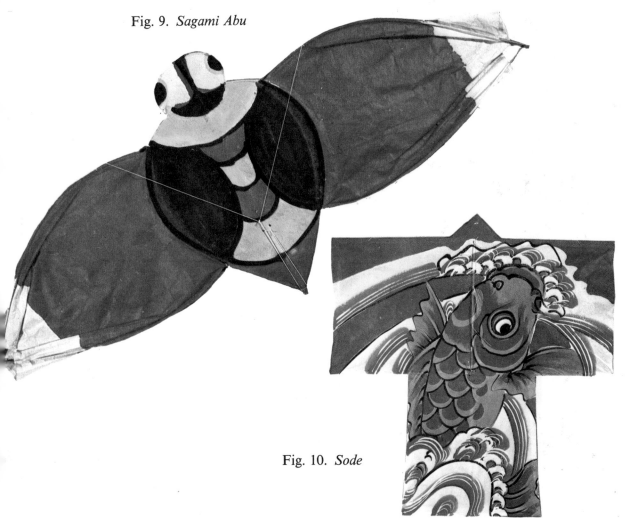

Fig. 10. *Sode*

19

Fig. 11. *Hachijo*
Fig. 12. *Rokkaku*

Fig. 13. *Beka*

Fig. 14. *Buka*

Fig. 15. *Bekkako*

Fig. 16. *Tomoe*

Fig. 17. *Suruga*

Fig. 18. *Sagara*

Fig. 19. *Machijirushi*

Fig. 20. *Machijirushi*

Fig. 21. *Munetaka*

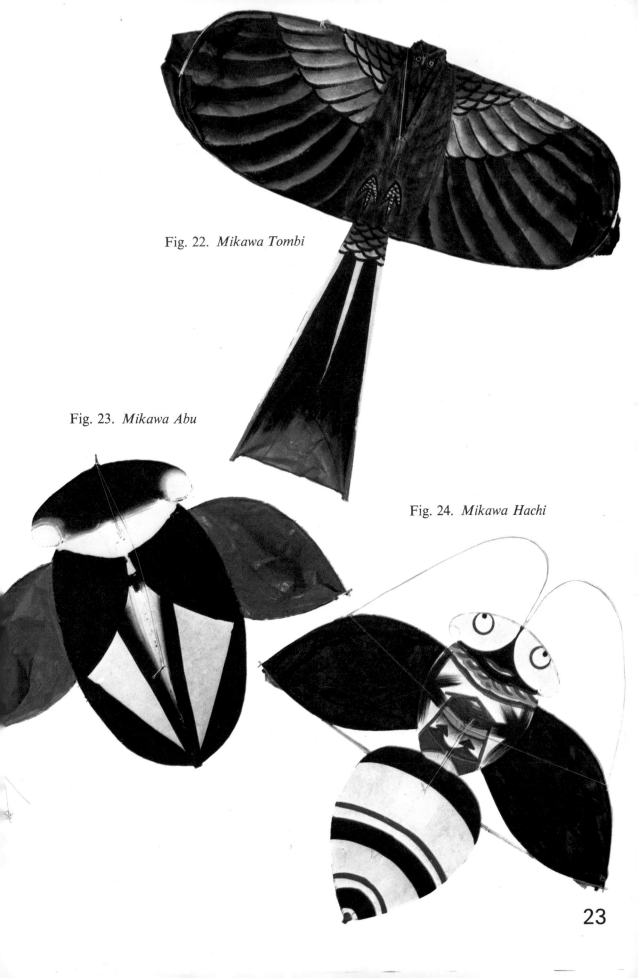

Fig. 22. *Mikawa Tombi*

Fig. 23. *Mikawa Abu*

Fig. 24. *Mikawa Hachi*

23

Fig. 25. *Kudoyama*

Fig. 26. *Kurayoshi*

Fig. 27. *Shojo*

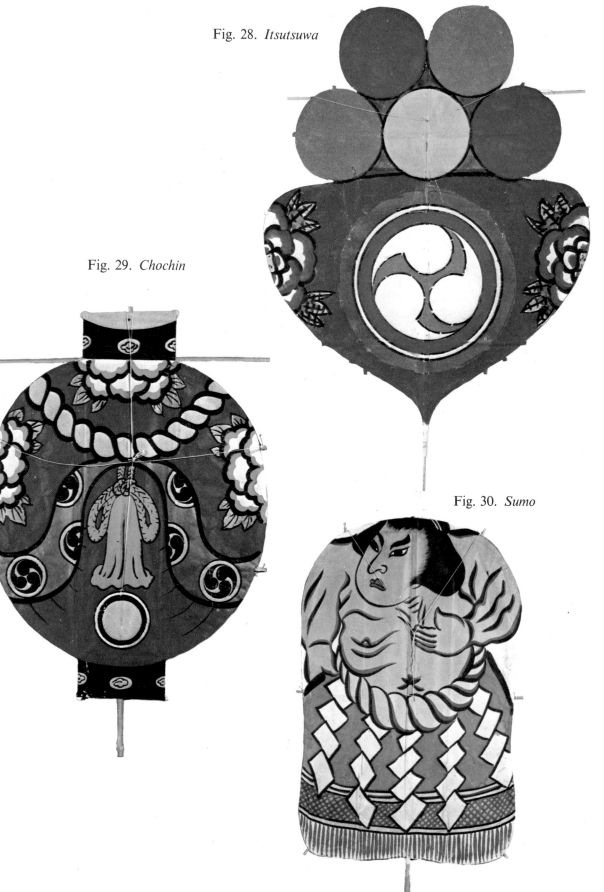

Fig. 28. *Itsutsuwa*

Fig. 29. *Chochin*

Fig. 30. *Sumo*

25

Fig. 31. *Mukade*

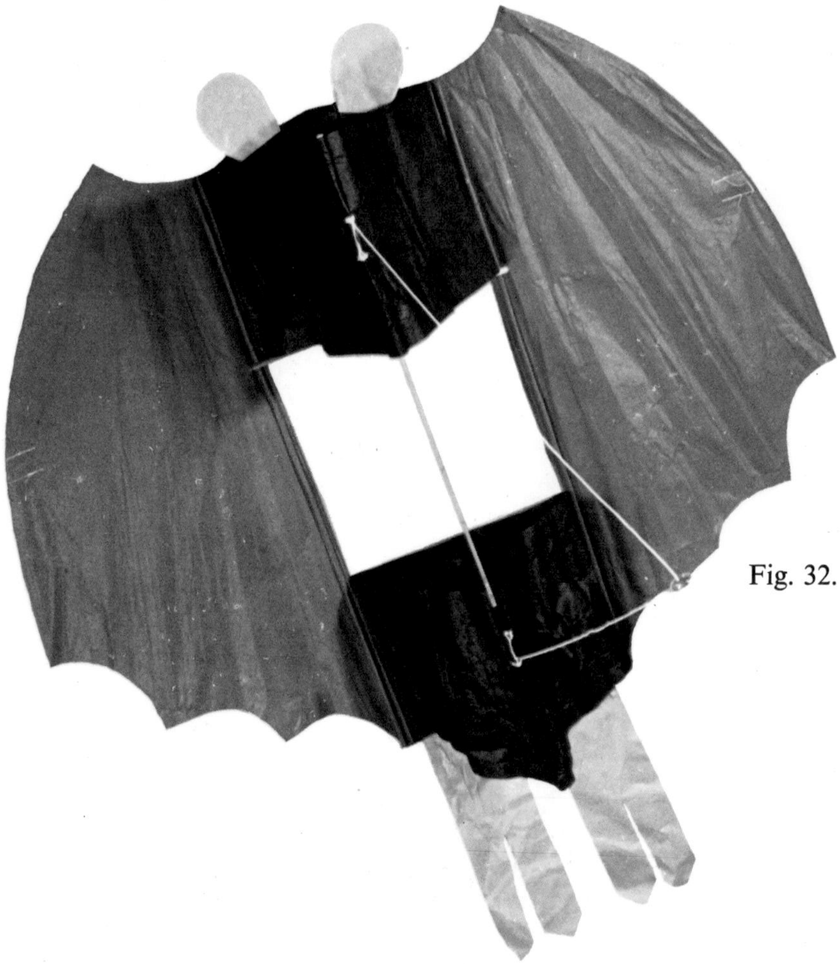

Fig. 32. *Komori*

Fig. 33. *Awa Yakko*

Fig. 34. *Tosa Jomon*

Fig. 35. *Matsuyama*

Fig. 36. *Nagasaki-hata*

Fig. 39. *Kappa*

Fig. 37. *Genji*

Fig. 38. *Heike*

Fig. 40. *Kizuki*

28

Fig. 41. *Tamana*

Fig. 42. *Kikusui*

Fig. 43. *Magoji*

Fig. 44. *Kaminari*

Fig. 45. *Yanagawa Karakasa Dojin*

Fig. 46. *Fukusuke Yakko*

30

Fig. 47. *Ura Yakko*

Fig. 48. *Goto Baramon*

Fig. 49. *Iki Kintoki*

31

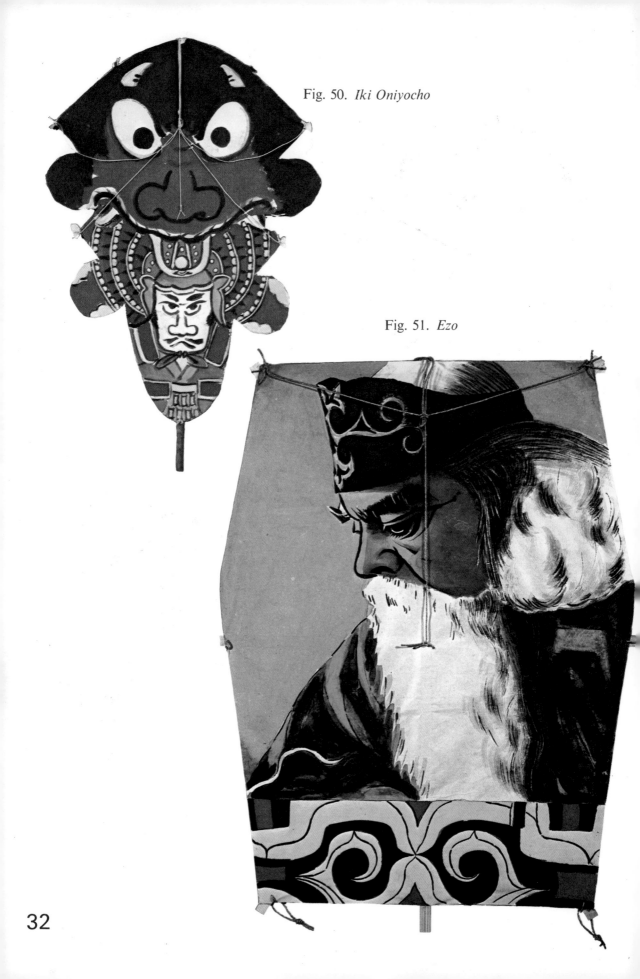

Fig. 50. *Iki Oniyocho*

Fig. 51. *Ezo*

Though Japanese kites were born in Edo and the great traditions of woodblock prints, Edo Nishiki (Brocade-picture) kites (Fig. 1), and Edo Ryu (Dragon) kites (Fig. 2) began there, today that city has become mammoth Tokyo, and the kite makers, who numbered roughly thirty-five shops before World War II, are now reduced to only one. The master of that shop, Takizo Hayashi, a government-designated living cultural property, feeling it his duty to pass to future generations the color schemes and brushwork styles he inherited from his ancestors, is diligently trying to keep the lamp of Edo kite culture burning.

My regional analysis of the Japanese kite begins in the northeast, the Tohoku, at the town of Hirosaki, which produces the Tsugaru kite (Fig. 3). The low winter temperatures in this area are fatal to bamboo; consequently, this among all Japanese kites is the only one to use thin strips of a kind of cypress in the framework. The paper is decorated with bright warrior paintings with a tradition of 200 years. The designs and workmanship are excellent enough to rank these among the best five Japanese folk toys. Roughly 100 miles east of Hirosaki, in the town of Hachinohe, workmen make the famous Nambu kites (Fig. 4), of which I have already spoken. The pictures on these kites are works of art, and when Japanese folk crafts were introduced into Europe, they were among the most popular articles.

Sendai, formerly a great castle town and seat of feudal power, once produced many fine kites, but I was able to find only a single reproduction based on the Ichimon Ten-hata kite (Fig. 5). The Onna Berabo kite (Fig. 6) of Akita and the Aizu Dojin kite (Fig. 7) of Wakamatsu city on the cold Japan Sea are supposed to ward off evil.

The Kanto District boasts the Oji Hibuse kite (Fig. 8), which is supposed to protect from fire, and the Sagami Abu kite (Fig. 9), made by the only female kite maker in Japan, as well as the jacket-shaped Sode kite (Fig. 10), from the Boso Peninsula in Chiba, which protects Tokyo Bay, An interesting legend is associated with the Hachijo Naga kite (Fig. 11) from Hachijojima, an island under the administration of Tokyo. In the early twelfth century, the true shogun, Minamoto Tametomo, and his small son were arrested and banished to Hachijojima. It is said that, in order to return his son to the mainland where he might inherit his rightful position, Tametomo made a large kite, put his son on it, and tearful at the parting, sent him across the water. For this reason, the Hachijo Naga kite always bears a picture of Tametomo.

On the Japan Sea side of the Chubu District, where kite contests are famous, octagonal shapes are the distinguishing characteristic (Fig. 12). On the Pacific side, along the famous Tokaido, however, kite makers specialize in unusual shapes: the Beka kite (Fig. 13) and the Buka kite (Fig. 14)—the former makes a sound like beka-beka and the latter one like buka-buka when raised—the conical Bekkako kite (Fig. 15), the comma-shaped Tomoe kite (Fig. 16), the Suruga kite (Fig. 17), with its wide variety of ornament and with outstanding flying capabilities that make it a favorite in contests, and the Sagara (Fig. 18), Hamamatsu Machijirushi (Fig. 19 and 20), and Munetaka kites (Fig. 21), all of which are designed to be good fliers.

Nagoya, the most important city in the Chubu District, produces many kites in shapes of birds or insects: the Mikawa Tombi (Fig.22)—(oddly enough named for a bird called the Siberian black kite), the Abu (Fig. 23) (gadfly), the Semi (cicada) and the Hachi (bee) kites (Fig. 24).

The Osaka-Kyoto region, second in size only to Tokyo, lacks kite makers today. Although in the past they are supposed to have produced some, perhaps the famous commercial minds of this area found kites a pastime beneath their consideration. Five miles to the south, however, in Wakayama, the Kudoyama kite (Fig. 25) and eleven miles to the north the Kurayoshi (Fig. 26) kites are produces.

The smallest of the main Japanese Islands, Shikoku, is still the nation's leading producer of fine kites. Some of their most famous specimens, each with a different shape and a different ornamental motif, include the Shojo (Fig. 27), the Itsutsuwa (Fig. 28), the Chochin (Fig. 29), and the Sumo kites (Fig. 30). All of these are works of folk art that can be enjoyed for their beauty alone. Other interesting kites from Shikoku are the

Master kite maker Takizo Hayashi checking one of his works.

Mukade (Fig. 31) (centipede) and Komori (Fig. 32) (bat) carefully constructed, multi-dimension, artistic deformations of the real animals.

The Awa Yakko kite (Fig. 33) is so striking that at the International Trade Fair, held in Tokyo in 1959, an American buyer ordered one million of them.

Tosa, maker of the finest paper in Japan, also produces an elegant kite called the Tosa Jomon (Fig. 34) as well as the Matsuyama kite (Fig. 35).

The area of greatest foreign influence on kite making, the southernmost island, Kyushu, is a treasure house of wonderful, many-shaped kites. For instance the Hata kites of Nagasaki (Fig. 36), the irregular rectangles of which are the special marks of such Kyushu kites as the Genji (Fig. 37), Heike (Fig. 38), Kappa (Fig. 39), Kizuki (Fig. 40), Tamana (Fig. 41), Kikusui (Fig. 42), and others. The Magoji kite (Fig. 43), masterpiece of the late kite maker Magojiro, is entertaining because the motifs are arranged to suggest a human face and a dragon at the same time. Sometimes it is difficult to tell one from the other. The Kaminari (thunder) kite (Fig. 44) is a childlike pictorial version of the Japanese tradition to the effect that a demon in the heavens causes thunder by beating drums. Unfortunately, no one today makes the romantic Chinese-style Yanagawa Karakasa Dojin kite (Fig. 45).

Kites in stylized human forms include the Fukusuke Yakko kite (Fig. 46) and the so-called reverse Yakko (Fig. 47) originally designed by a maker of swords and horse trappings whose business failure caused him to become a kite designer. This clever devise, perhaps the result of the maker's inability to paint faces, shows only the back of the man shape, which, when aloft, seems to march bravely through the sky.

Fukusuke Sode   *Iwai*

Kites from the islands near Kyushu include the Baramon kite (Fig. 48) of Goto and the Kintoki (Fig. 49) and Oniyocho (Fig. 50) kites of Ikishima, showing a demon with a helmet in the style of the traditional Japanese warrior kites. The framework of this particular kite is the most elaborate to be found in Japan.

In my review of the kites of Japan I have mentioned none from the northernmost island, Hokkaido, because, until the colonization and development movement of one hundred years ago, this area remained backward. To celebrate their centennial, however, the people of Hokkaido have developed their first kite, called Ezo, the old name for the island. The designer, poet Hikozo Ota, has the following comment to make.

"I have made the kite form hexagonal to resemble the shape of Hokkaido (Fig. 51). The pictorial design represents an Ainu chief lamenting to the gods the decline of his people. Thus, though the Ezo is the newest of all Japanese kites, its design symbolizes a people whose ancestors inhabited these islands before the Japanese themselves arrived here."

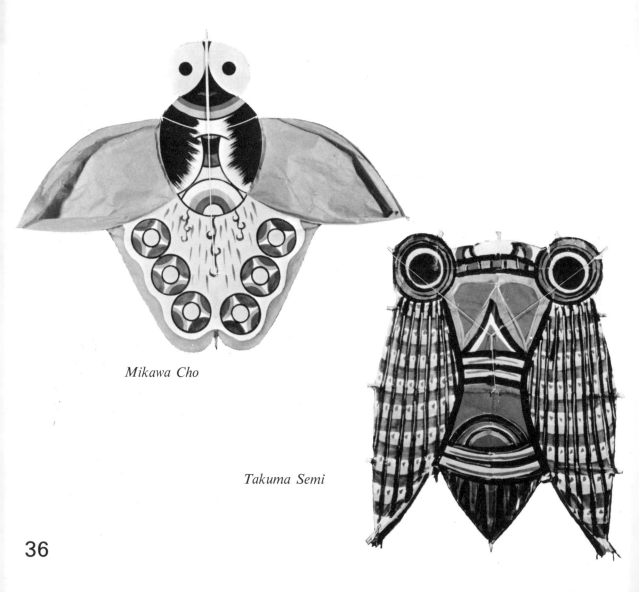

Mikawa Cho

Takuma Semi

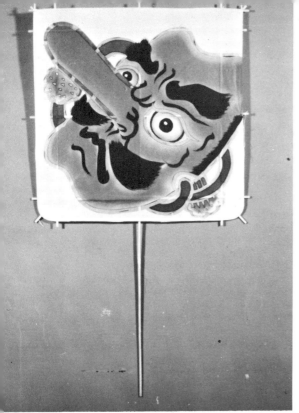

Machijirushi   *Sanjo Rokkaku*

Traditional Kite Games

To increase the enjoyment of flying kites the Japanese have developed certain games with set rules. For instance, in Sanjo, on the Japan Sea, the young men gather in two groups, one on either side of the river that runs through the town, and using from thirty to fifty people in each team, raise Sanjo Rokkaku kites measuring from nine to eleven feet in height. The goal of the game is to entangle the line of the opposing kite with one's own line and, by means of friction, to cut its cord and force it to fall to the river flats. A kind of rugby match then ensues to capture the fallen kite.

At Hamamatsu, on the Pacific Coast, each of the sixty-six block divisions of the town makes kites bearing their block symbol and ranging in size from sixteen to twenty-six feet. Flying them at the appointed battle field, each block team regards all kites other than those of its own group as the enemy—or sometimes only as an easy mark. To the rhythmical battle cries of shouts and calls, teams of fifty people, working as a single unit, mount their kites till the lines are fully extended and then, controlling the kite by means of a portable winch, attack the kites of other blocks and, try to cut their lines by a tactic of entanglement. This can be achieved either by bringing one's line on top of that of the opponent's kite or by raising one's own line from below. At the command of the team leader, each group works from front boun-

37

Kite contest at Hamamatsu.

dary to rear boundary and from right and left across the battle field frantically striving to down all comers. Becoming too absorbed in the offensive, however, can cause loss of control of the kite. The game is difficult but exhilarating, and a kite whose cord has been cut, sailing and dipping on the wind as it flies toward Mount Fuji, crimson in the dying light of the evening, creates a beautiful, thoroughly Japanese picture.

Nagasaki competition kites carry heavy armor. Although, at a glance, the kite string looks perfectly ordinary, in fact, at from thirty to sixty feet in front of the kite itself, the line is wrapped in linen, or sometimes wire, coated with a compound of a paste-like substance and ground glass. In addition, from numerous spots along the line project small scythe-like metal blades. Since the kites are small —from one to three feet in diameter— and employ only two vertical strings, which make them tend to dip easily, a skilful operator can send his kite rising or falling with great speed. In times gone by, groups of merrymakers would flock to hillsides, spread their straw mats, open their lunches, and while tippling sake happily together, enjoy the kite fights. Today they do nearly the same thing, but in convertible automobiles.

The strictest rule governing these fights is that the loser must

Wanwan

Nagasaki-hata

bear no grudge. Ill feelings must not linger until the following day; instead the battle must create between the combatants a link that should develop into friendship. This attitude of bloodthirsty battle contrasted by a sense of tranquility is typical of the southern part of Japan.

The largest kite in Japan—and probably in the world—is the Wanwan kite built on the island of Tokushima, in the warm Pacific waters off the shores of Shikoku. This monster, consisting of 2,500 sheets of Japanese paper, has a diameter of sixty-five feet and weighs 1,700 pounds. Its tail is made of tens of lengths of thick ship rope bundled together. Heavy anchors buried in the ground prevent it from flying away, and a winch reels out its line and controls its movement. Before World War II, yearly, in May, this great kite was flown in the strong sea winds, but it flies no more.

The largest kite in Japan.

Formerly Japan's second largest, but with the passing of the Wanwan, the largest, is the fifty-by-thirty-five-foot kite, flown in the town of Hojubana, about one hour's car ride north of Tokyo. Large numbers of young people, working in groups of one hundred and using ropes more than one and one-half inches in diameter, used to have such vicious battles with these huge kites that frequent injuries prompted the police and the town council to limit the number of kites permitted to two at a time and to demand gentlemanly behavior on the parts of the fliers. Under these modified terms, the great kites fly even today.

To double the thrills experienced by the competitive kite fliers on the ground, designers have devised a bow made of bamboo or

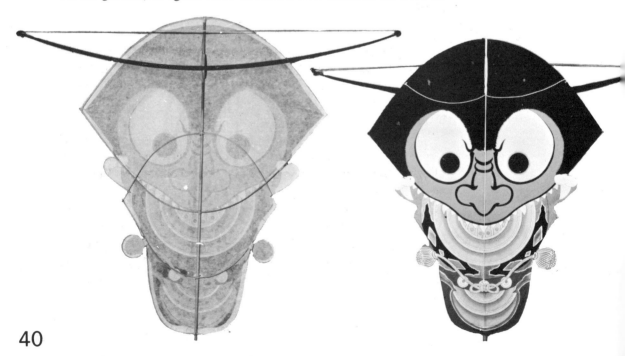

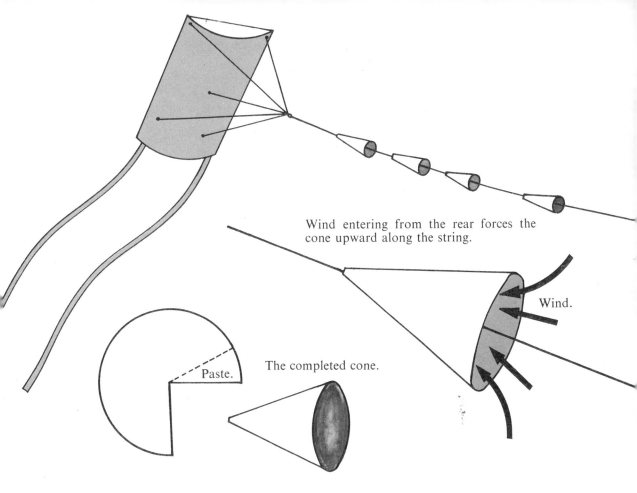

Wind entering from the rear forces the cone upward along the string.

Wind.

Paste.

The completed cone.

some strong wood with a strip of wisteria-vine bark stretched tight from end to end. This is attached to the top of the kite, from side to side, so that when the kite is in the air the vibrations make the bark emit a sound that is reverberated by the kite paper as by a sounding board. The extra excitement this produces is similar to the effect of removing mufflers from racing cars. Although different parts of the country claim that other noise-maker materials are better than wisteria, all of them are so loud that the government forbade their use during the World War II, because the sounds they make could be easily mistaken for the whistling of enemy bombs.

This year, I noticed some children in a Tokyo suburb playing at cable cars with their kites. They did this by making small cones of thin red, blue, and yellow paper, opening a hole in the pointed end, and slipping the string of a flying kite through them. The little colored cones, as they gradually moved up toward the kite, looked very much like the scenic cable cars used in mountainous country. Though this game is new, it closely resembles the principle employed in the Kyoto Hi-no-maru kite and the Hanagasa kite of Tokyo. In these cases, an umbrella-like frame of paper and bamboo ribs is filled with paper flowers or flowered tapes and secured in a half-closed position by a loop of thin paper. It is then slid on the string of a flying kite through a hole in the umbrella end. Wind

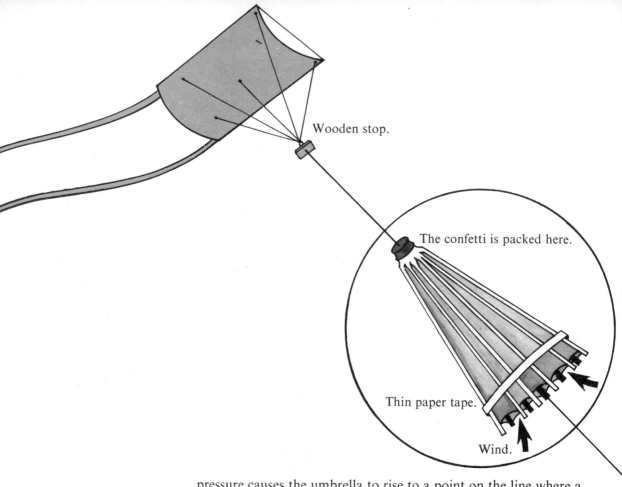

Wooden stop.

The confetti is packed here.

Thin paper tape.

Wind.

pressure causes the umbrella to rise to a point on the line where a pre-set disc stops it. The wind is still blowing, however, and its force driving into the umbrella breaks the thin paper tape, opens the umbrella completely, and showers the ground with a snow storm of bright flowers.

Try your hand at these traditional and distinctive Japanese group and individual kite games. I am sure that you will enjoy them.

Making a Japanese Kite

Of all the various forms of Japanese kites, I have selected the standard rectangular one to explain because it is so simple that even a small child can easily make and fly it.

Preparations

Framework: Several thin strips of bamboo about two feet long. If these are unavailable, use light, flexible plastic rods or some light wood.

Paper: Japanese paper (one and one-half by two feet) is best, but if you cannot obtain it, find some other, thin, lightweight, strong paper.

Daruma

Picture: Paint any picture you like, but paint it before you assemble the kite. Once the paper is on the frame, painting is difficult.

Glue: Craft glues are suitable, but we Japanese usually mix flour and water and boil it till it is smooth in texture. The resulting paste is light, smooth, and goes on well.

String: A thin string to bind the framework is essential, as well as a tougher thicker string for flying.

Miscellaneous: In addition to these materials you will want a measure, a knife, scissors, a triangle, paints, brushes, and an atomizer for spraying a light mist of water.

The Framework

Line up three strips of bamboo vertically and five horizontally; the distances among them must be equal, and they must all intersect at right angles. Add two diagonal pieces which intersect at the kite center, and tie the pieces together as Diagram 1 indicates.

Next, tie a piece of string at point A, and winding it around each of the horizontal ribs on that side, finally tie the other end at point B. Repeat the process on the other side: run the string from point C to point D. To make the tabs for pasting on the paper, cut V-shaped notches, one inch deep, in the four corners, fold the tabs inward along the dotted lines in Diagram 2. Also cut small holes in the folds you just made at points corresponding to the ribs in the framework. The ribs should jut out slightly when the paper is pasted on the frame.

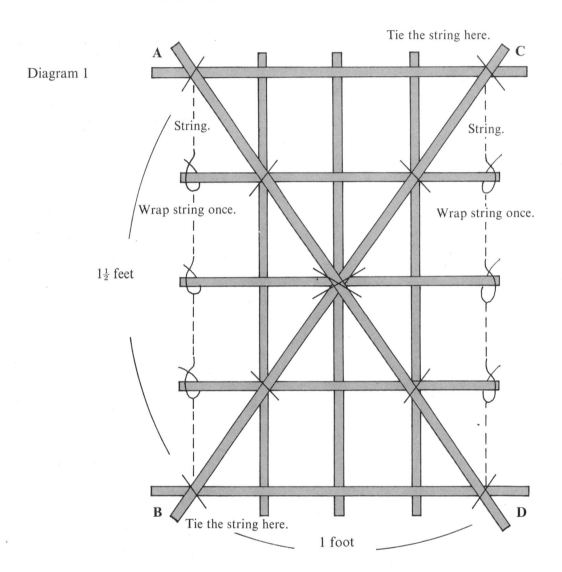

Diagram 1

Tie the string here.

A

C

String.

String.

Wrap string once.

Wrap string once.

1½ feet

B

D

Tie the string here.

1 foot

Pasting on the Paper

Apply an even coat of paste to all the framework members; next spread a coat on the tabs of the kite paper. Work fast, for the paste dries quickly. Beginning at the top of the kite and making sure that the vertical ribs jut through the holes in the paper, fold the paste tab over toward the rear. Then pull the paper down and to the right and left so that no wrinkles form. Fold the right and left

44

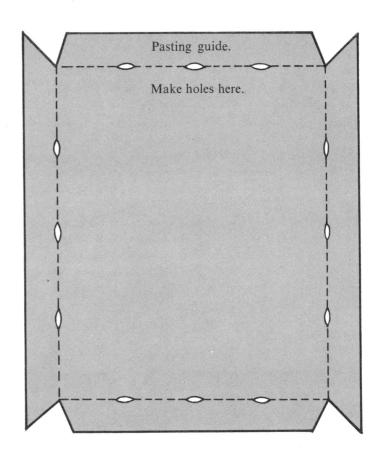

Pasting guide.

Make holes here..

Diagram 2

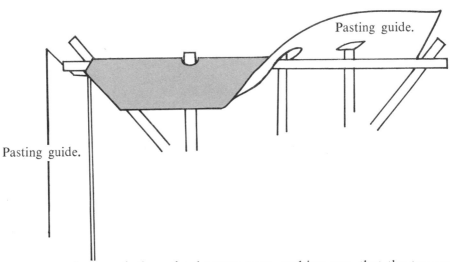

Pasting guide.

Pasting guide.

flaps and then the bottom ones, making sure that the top and bottom ribs and the strings on the right and left go as far into the folds as possible. Pasting the paper on requires an amount of skill. In fact, a Japanese kite maker's reputation hangs on this ability.

Diagram 3

Bowing the Kite

When the paper is on nicely, fill the atomizer with water, and spray a fine mist on the back of the kite. Do not soak the paper; a light spray is all that is required to remove all small wrinkles and lumps. Now stand the kite in a shaded, well ventilated place to dry. When the kite is thoroughly dry, after tying strings on the projecting ribs on the right and left sides of the top and bottom, bow it to the extent shown in Diagram 3. Do not bend it too much.

Now that you have finished your Japanese kite, take it outside and fly it.

The Kite's Principle of Flight

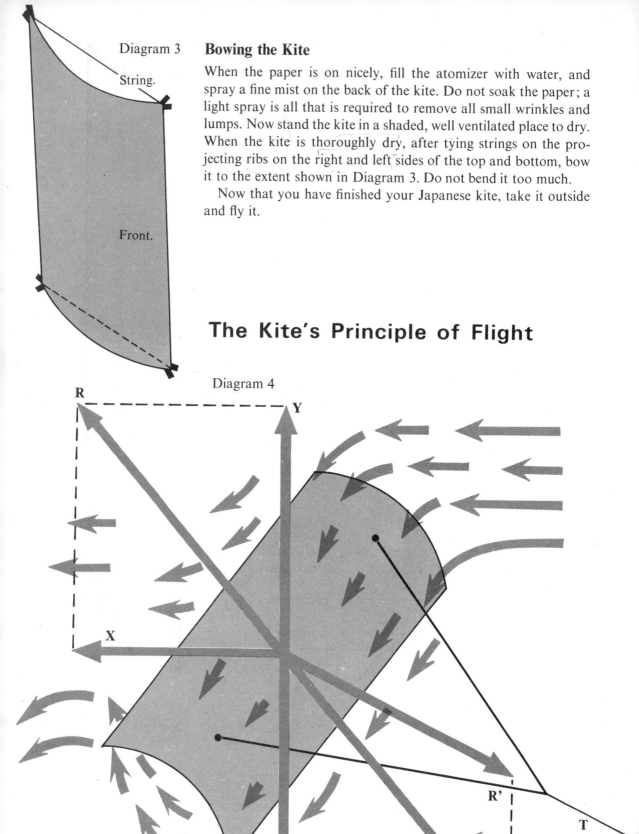

Diagram 4

Wind flowing in the direction of the arrows, striking the kite, flows downward and thus creates air pressure, which causes the kite to rise (see Diagram 4).

Wind blowing across the top of the kite also tends to make it rise.

I will call the lifting force Y, the force driving the kite sidewards X, and the combination of these two forces R. When R', the combination of W, the kite weight, and T, the tug on the string, balances R, the kite stands motionless in air.

Addition of a tail and of guide strings causes a real kite to fly at an angle.

Skill in Flying a Kite

Balance

Using a measure to compensate for the surprising inaccuracy of the human eye, make sure the center of the kite is the actual center. Not even a slight discrepancy is permissible.

Next, hold the kite lightly to check the weight balance. If you have repaired the kite paper with a small patch on one side, it is essential to put another similar patch on the other side. If a little extra string is wound around one of the ribs, a compensatory amount must be added to the opposite side.

Because bamboo is resilient it is possible to adjust the bow of Japanese kites to suit wind conditions: strong bow for strong winds, slight bow for light winds. When the kite is not in use, slacken the bowing strings till the kite is perfectly flat, or the bamboo will loose its resilience.

Guide Strings

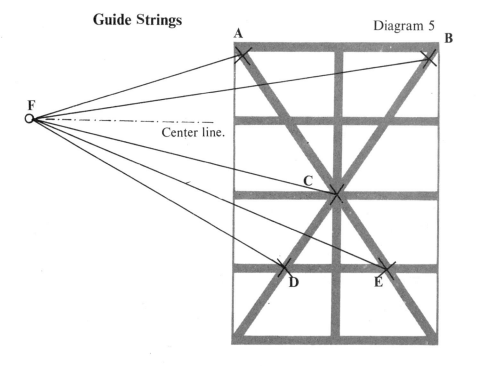

Diagram 5

Center line.

The proper attachment of the guide strings is of the utmost importance to the way a kite flies. Although individual methods and varying numbers of strings exist for different kite shapes, I will explain that for the standard rectangular kite.

As you see in Diagram 5, point F, where all the guide strings join, must fall half the way between the middle and top of the kite. Point F must also, as you see in Diagram 6, fall midway between A and B and midway between D and E, on the line C. If point C is high, the kite will fly well; if it is low, the kite will not rise high, no matter how much string you let out. The placement in Diagram 7 will make the kite fly high and as shown in Diagram 8. The high placement of string C (shown in Diagram 9) will let the kite fly far and fast on windy days.

Sometimes a kite tends to lean to one side or to spin. Since this may be the result of a momentary current, check the situation thoroughly before doing anything, but if the fault seems to be in the kite, shorten the string on the side away from the direction of turn. Do this by simple wrapping the string once around the rib (see Diagram 10).

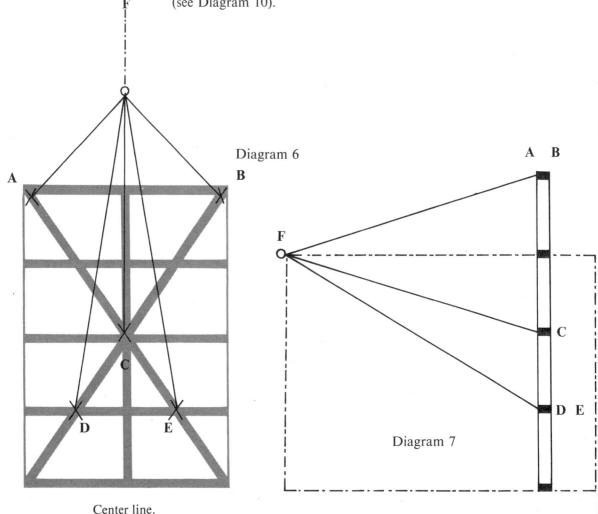

Diagram 6

Diagram 7

Center line.

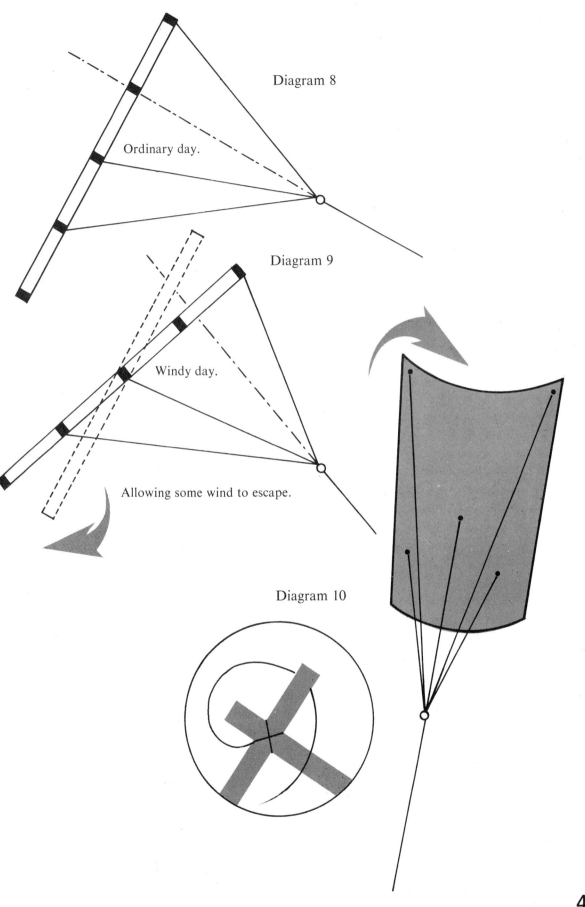

Diagram 8

Ordinary day.

Diagram 9

Windy day.

Allowing some wind to escape.

Diagram 10

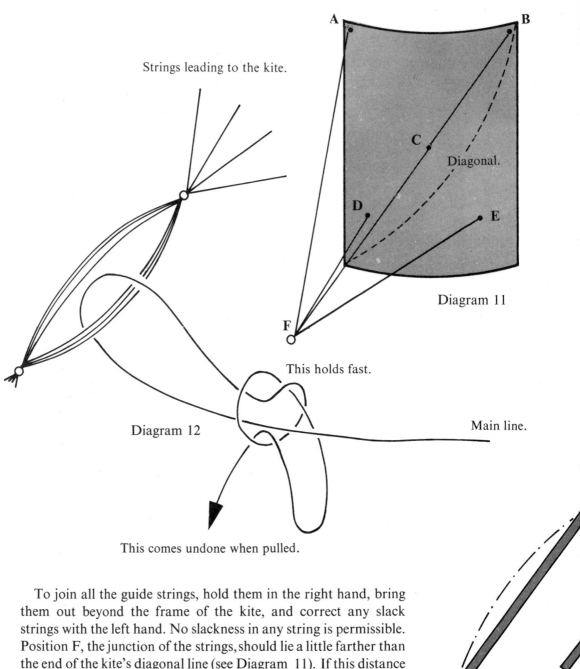

Strings leading to the kite.

A

B

C

Diagonal.

D

E

Diagram 11

F

This holds fast.

Diagram 12

Main line.

This comes undone when pulled.

To join all the guide strings, hold them in the right hand, bring them out beyond the frame of the kite, and correct any slack strings with the left hand. No slackness in any string is permissible. Position F, the junction of the strings, should lie a little farther than the end of the kite's diagonal line (see Diagram 11). If this distance is too short, the kite will spin instead of rising.

Knot the strings at F in two places to form a loop through which it is convenient to pass the string used to fly the kite. For instance, with the help of this devise adjustments and removal of the flying string are easy. Furthermore, it provides more slack to help you work loose a kite caught in a tree (see Diagram 12).

Attaching the Tail

Select something strong and light—Japanese paper, for instance —and make a long tail. The usual is three times the length of the kite's diagonal. A rule of thumb to follow in tail adjustments

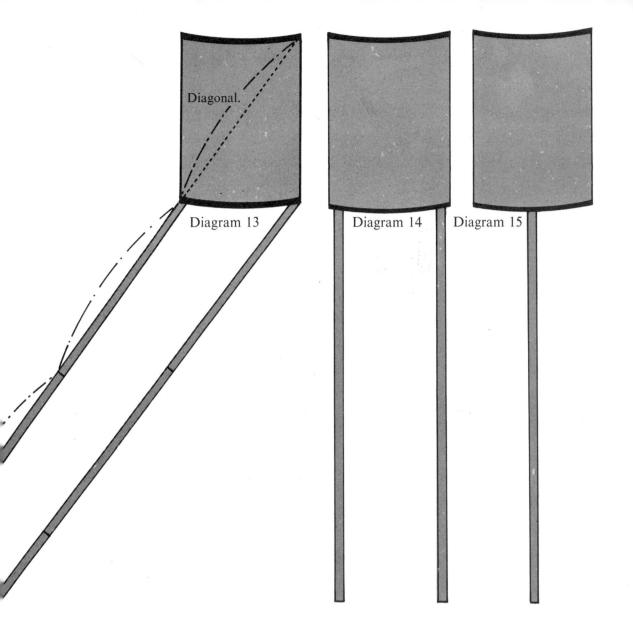

Diagonal.

Diagram 13   Diagram 14   Diagram 15

is long for windy days, short for calm days (Diagram 13). At the beginning, attach a tail four times the length of the kite diagonal, and gradually adjust it to suit the wind conditions. Do not forget, however, that the higher the kite rises, the more susceptible it becomes to winds that are not apparent on the ground. Consequently, do not over-shorten the tail at first try, because, even should such a kite rise, once it gets into the higher air, where stronger winds blow, it will come straight down again.

Of the many ways of attaching the tail, that in Diagram 14 with balanced sections on the right and left is the standard. The attachment in Diagram 15 is for fairly windy days and sudden rising and diving. That in Diagram 16 has a small wooden weight added to a cord that makes the tail swing back and forth like a

51

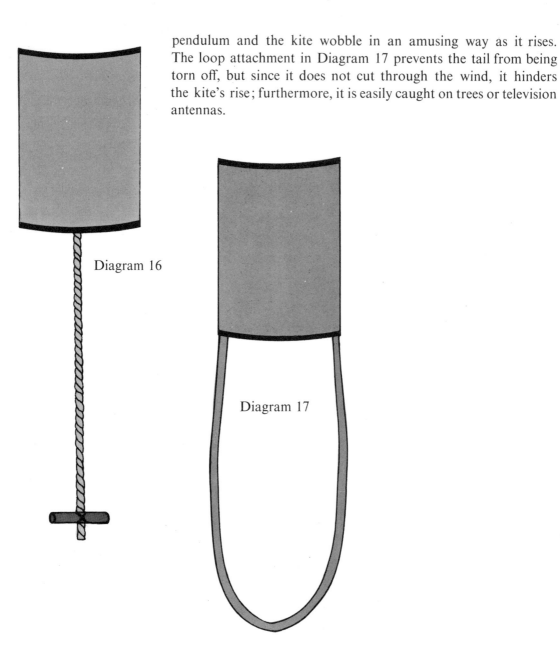

pendulum and the kite wobble in an amusing way as it rises. The loop attachment in Diagram 17 prevents the tail from being torn off, but since it does not cut through the wind, it hinders the kite's rise; furthermore, it is easily caught on trees or television antennas.

Diagram 16

Diagram 17

Sending the Kite Aloft

Shingo Modegi, the sixty-seven year old owner of one of the best restaurants in Tokyo, has captured trophies and awards at all of the nation's most important kite meets. A recognized authority, he receives numerous letters asking for advice from kite-fanciers all over the country. In 1966, packing several kites in his luggage, he traveled to France to fulfill a life-long dream: flying a kite from the top of the Eifel Tower. The Paris newspapers commented on the devotion of this man to his dream and his hobby.

Japanese kites being flown at the Eifel Tower.

Shingo Modegi and a young French friend prepare to fly a kite.

When asked the most important thing in putting a kite aloft, Mr. Modegi always says, "Remain calm, and proceed in an orderly, accurate fashion." He goes on to remark that when in Paris attempting to raise a kite before a group of curious onlookers, his natural reaction was to become agitated and nervous. He overcame this danger, however, and was successful in raising his kite because he deliberately calmed himself by taking about twenty minutes to make thorough preparations.

Once you have arrived at the field or park where you are going to fly your kite, take plenty of time to recheck balance and the conditions of the guide strings. Rushing will only cause damage to your kite. If the exterior appearance seems in good order, let out a little string, and throw the kite lightly upward to further check balance. Correct any slight tendency to incline by adjusting the tail and guide strings. Next, if the wind conditions are good, proceeding as you did in the test, throw the kite lightly up, and letting the string out gradually, send it aloft. On calm days, have someone hold the kite high over his head, until a good breeze comes along.

Never try to raise a kite by running along the ground because

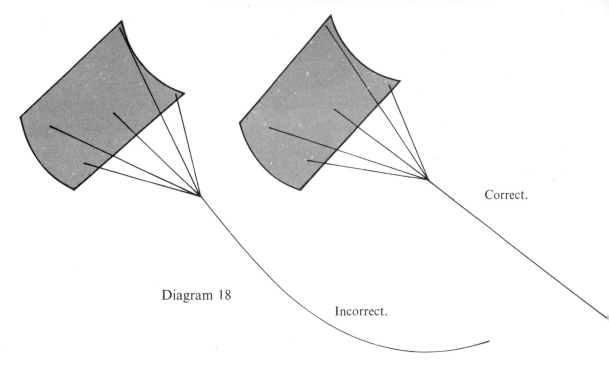

Correct.

Diagram 18

Incorrect.

doing so causes minor damage which will make it always neces-
sary to run in order to put the kite in the air.

The tail should always lie in front of the kite, and if it catches
in weeds or brush, the person raising the kite, since he is closer
than the helper, should disentangle it immediately.

After the kite is up, you have a chance to show how skillful you
are. Once again, remain calm, and be serious about your work.

To make the kite go higher, coordinating your action with the
wind, draw the string toward you in short pulls. To correct ten-
dencies to dance right or left or to tip over, slacken the string.
Though the kite will then fly off temporarily, it will soon right
itself and, riding on an air current, will remain so stable that you
could tie the string to a tree root and forget it.

Limits to which you can reel out string depend on the size of
the kite and the strength of the wind. In Diagram 18 you see
examples of proper and improper string control. A light string
prohibits extreme distances in flying; one that is too heavy for
the kite will sag so that either you step on it or it catches in
something.

Another point to remember is the necessity of always leaving
a little string in reserve on the reel in your hand. No matter how
well your kite is flying, the time may come when you need to
make corrections in its flight, and without reserve of line, you will
be unable to do so.

It is possible to fly a kite at maximum altitudes by running
toward it after you have let out as much string as you safely can.
By approaching the point on the ground directly under the kite
you shorten the distance between it and you and, therefore,
increase the vertical altitude possible with a limited amount of
line.

55

Finally, I will make a few comments about precautions to observe in bringing a kite down. Kite master Modegi says that you should always bring kites down slowly as if you were having a pleasant conversation with them. In other words, without snapping or jerking, reel in line three times, and let in out once, always keeping an eye on wind conditions. Chat with the kite—as the little boy in the preface did—and ask, "How are things? Are you getting along all right? Come down now, and we'll go home. You can go for another fly tomorrow."

Remember, the resistance is greater on a kite being lowered than on one being raised or on one in flight; consequently, the danger of damage or deformation increases. Mr. Modegi says, "The part of kite flying that demands the greatest care, is bringing them in safely."

A Few Interesting Kite Shapes and Frames

Different kite shapes require various framework assemblies. Why not try your hand with a few of these?

NOTE: To make the framework easy to understand, I have used heavy lines to represent the structure. Remember, however, that kite frames must be light and slender.

The Hirado Karakuri Kintoki Kite

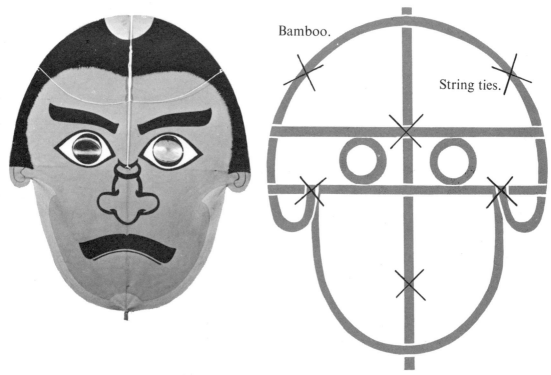

Bamboo.

String ties.

Use slender, resilient strips of bamboo. Leave holes for the eyes, and insert eyeballs on axes that will twirl round in the wind.

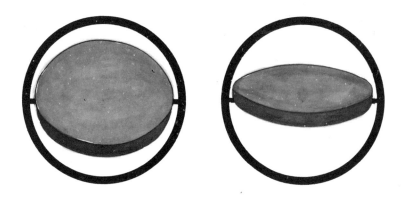

The Hata Kite

The outside frame is string pasted inside the peripheral fold. Make the tassels by cutting slits about two thirds the width of a strip of paper, winding the strips lightly, and tying them to the frame string.

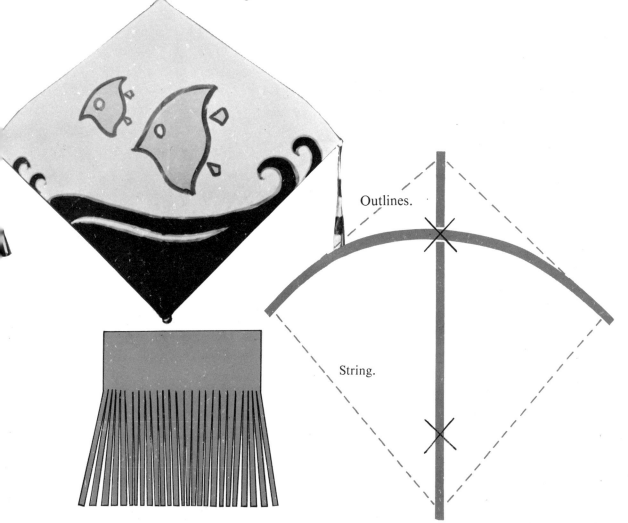

Outlines.

String.

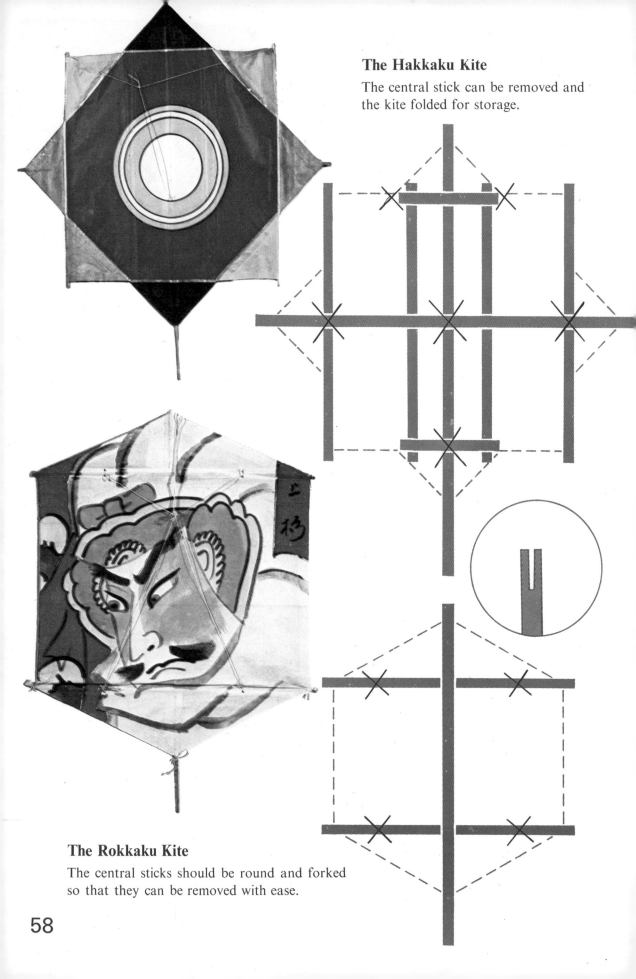

The Hakkaku Kite

The central stick can be removed and the kite folded for storage.

The Rokkaku Kite

The central sticks should be round and forked so that they can be removed with ease.

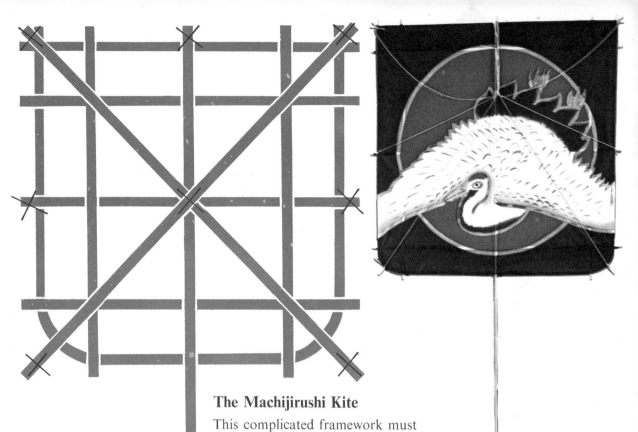

The Machijirushi Kite

This complicated framework must be both strong and light.

The Tsugaru Kite

Use thin strips of resilient, strong cypress instead of bamboo for this kite.

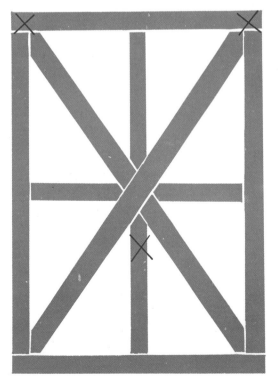

The Tombi Kite

Fold the wing tips along the framework, but leave a small opening so that wind can pass through.

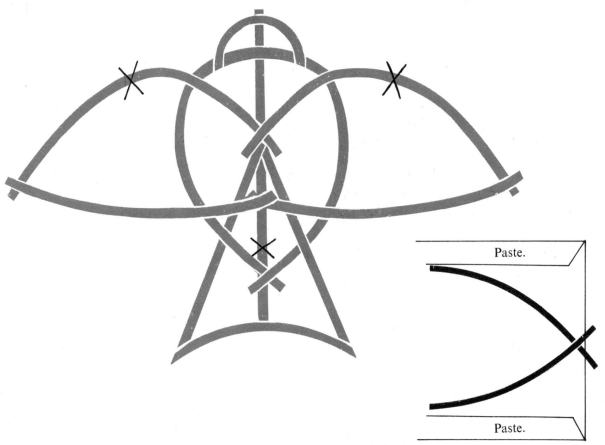

Paste.

Paste.

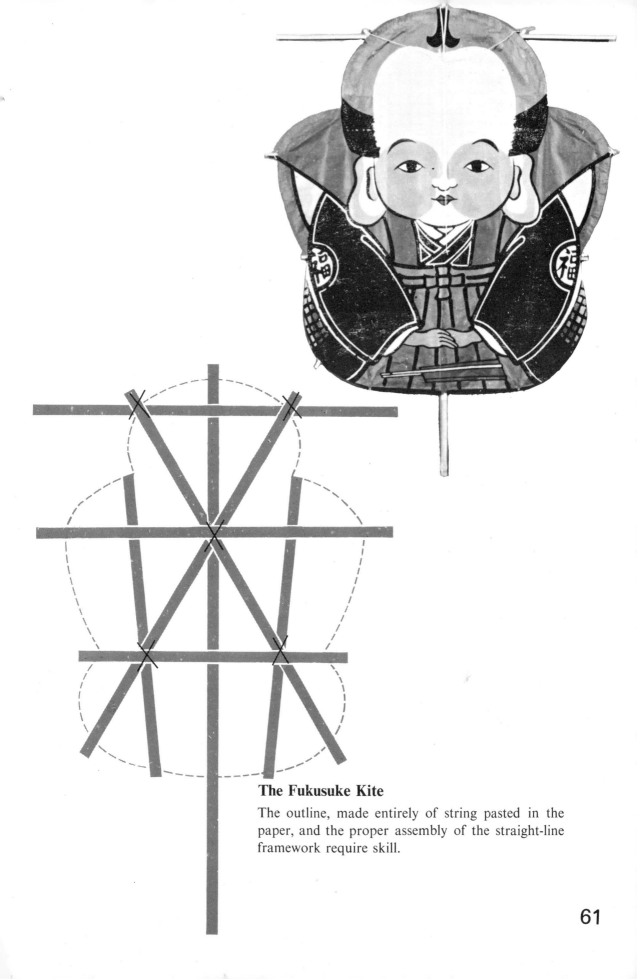

The Fukusuke Kite

The outline, made entirely of string pasted in the
paper, and the proper assembly of the straight-line
framework require skill.

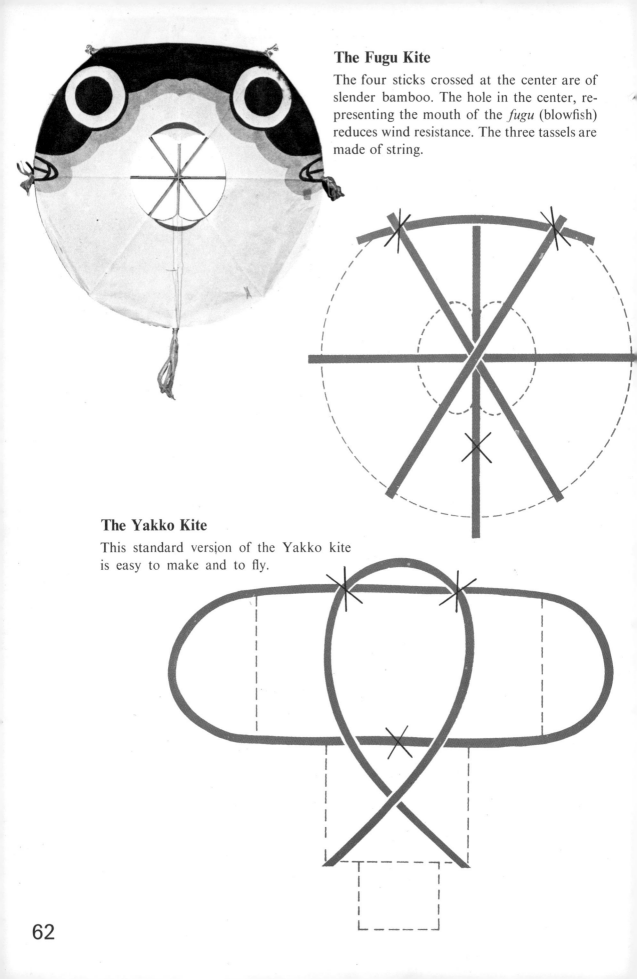

The Fugu Kite

The four sticks crossed at the center are of slender bamboo. The hole in the center, representing the mouth of the *fugu* (blowfish) reduces wind resistance. The three tassels are made of string.

The Yakko Kite

This standard version of the Yakko kite is easy to make and to fly.

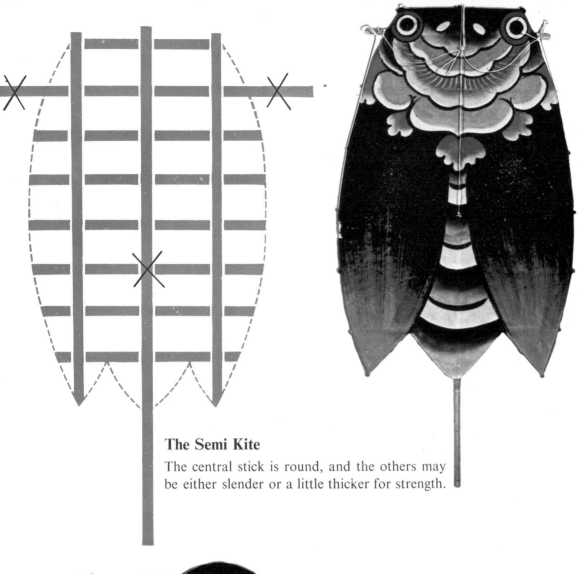

The Semi Kite

The central stick is round, and the others may be either slender or a little thicker for strength.